Beginning
with Babies

**Mary Lou Kinney and
Patricia Witt Ahrens**

 **Redleaf Press**®
www.redleafpress.org
800-423-8309

Published by Redleaf Press
10 Yorkton Court
St. Paul, MN 55117
www.redleafpress.org

Printed in the United States of America

Library of Congress Cataloging-in-Publication Data
Kinney, Mary Lou, 1947–
       Beginning with babies / by Mary Lou Kinney and Patricia Witt Ahrens.
              p.   cm.
       Includes bibliographical references.
       ISBN 978-1-929610-04-4
       1. Day care centers—Activity programs. 2. Family day care—Activity programs.
3. Infants—Development. 4. Early childhood education—Activity programs.
I. Ahrens, Patricia Witt, 1950– II. Title.

  HQ778.5 .K56 2001
  362.71′2—dc21   2001019533

Printed on acid-free paper

We dedicate this book to our mothers,
Betty Seidl and Millie Witt, who were our first teachers.

Acknowledgments

This book represents knowledge and insight gathered from our combined twenty-five years of teaching and observing young children and from the extraordinary child care/early childhood professionals who, through their enthusiasm, wisdom, and commitment, support children's important early learning.

Our gratitude goes to our families, friends, and colleagues who provided support and encouragement throughout the writing of this book.

A special thanks goes to our editor, Beth Wallace, for her patience and guidance.

Contents

Introduction

If you are a caregiver of babies who range in age from birth to fifteen months, this book is for you! We know your days are often isolating as well as physically and emotionally exhausting. The recent public-awareness campaigns about new research into how the brain develops and the importance of the early years in the child's lifelong development may create more questions for you from parents as they leave their baby in your care.

The potential for learning and development is dramatic during these first fifteen months of the baby's life. It is important that you have a basic understanding of what current thinking tells us about how babies develop. Equally important is your ability to translate that information to parents through the activities that you provide for their child. This book is meant to be a resource to help you do just that.

With the unfolding information about the brain, we now know that genetics ("nature") and environmental interaction ("nurture") both have an impact on a child's learning and development. Children are born with all the brain cells that they will ever have, but they lack the connections or "wiring" between those cells. The interplay between nature and nurture makes those connections in the baby's brain. In a nurturing environment (like your child care setting), a consistent and skilled caregiver (that would be you!) offers activities that stimulate the baby's brain and help develop the baby's senses and personality. So the care you give each baby plays a very big role in how the brain is "wired." When babies are in a negative environment where they are ignored, neglected, and not respected as special and unique people, the impact on their growth and development is serious and lifelong.

In this book, we have compiled a host of simple activities that you can do with babies. These activities are in sync with what we have learned from the research about the brain. From the time babies are newborns, the experiences they take in through their senses build the connections that help them learn and develop. Therefore, these activities are grouped by the development of the five senses, which are key to a baby's learning and growth. Each activity includes a list of the materials (if any) you will need, what you should do or how you should interact with the baby, and a brief explanation of how the activity contributes to the baby's overall development.

We hope the easy format of this book will help you with your daily caregiving and enrich your frequent communication with parents. Since you, as the caregiver, "partner" with parents to encourage their child's learning and development, it is only natural that you will want to share these activities so parents can continue them at home.

We loudly applaud you for the important work that you do. We look forward to the day when our society will acknowledge your work with the recognition and compensation that it deserves. We hope this book offers you a wealth of new thoughts and ideas for your caregiving of babies.

What Are Some Important Areas to Consider When Caring for Babies?

Many caregivers say they chose the job because they simply "love babies." Love is a valued factor that leads many to enter and stay in the caregiving profession. However, just loving babies is not enough. It's what you do with those loving feelings that counts. Because you love the babies, rather than just "winging it" when you care for them, you develop your skills and knowledge to best promote each child's learning and growth. Because parents trust you and the babies depend on you, you think through some important aspects of your caregiving practices. These areas include:

- Setting up a safe and healthy environment
- Engaging and communicating with parents
- Establishing routines and rituals
- Supporting each baby's developmental journey

Setting Up a Safe and Healthy Environment

Safety is a huge factor in the lives of babies! Thousands of babies are injured each year because of unsafe equipment, materials, and environments. Your local child care resource and referral agency, health department, hospital, fire department, and state or local child care licensing agency are just some of the valuable contacts you can use to prepare a safe and healthy environment for babies. Their resources may consist of checklists, free materials, plenty of technical assistance, and additional contacts. Remember, you will need to increase your vigilant attention to babies' safety as they grow older and become more mobile.

You can develop a safety checklist by thinking of the places where babies spend their awake and asleep time:

- Baby crib—Is it away from windows and loose window-shade cords?
- Playpen—Is the space between the mesh or slats too wide?
- Walker—Is it in good repair?
- Floor—Is the rug or floor clean? Are the electrical outlets covered?
- Outdoor space—Are there any small objects in the area that could cause choking?
- Buggy or stroller—Can the baby be strapped in easily?
- Diaper changing areas—Is a sink (for washing hands) located close to the changing area?

Engaging and Communicating with Parents

New parents are often pressed for time. They are making transitions in their lives, and if they have other children, they are helping siblings adjust to the new baby. They are looking to you for both support and information. The more parents and caregivers talk *and listen* to each other, the easier it is on everyone—especially the child. Parents and caregivers should talk daily about the baby's temperament, eating interests, sleep patterns, activity level, and special daily challenges and events. Parents can provide information for the caregiver like, "His grandma is here this week, and she likes to take him on daily stroller rides." The caregiver can offer valuable information to parents, such as "We played Celtic music today, and your son kicked his legs in rhythm with the music."

Here are some simple strategies that we have seen caregivers use to keep open the lines of communication with parents:

- Recent pictures of the babies and their families displayed in the baby room
- Pictures of the babies and their families put in a resealable plastic bag and made part of the storybook that is "read" to them each day. (Refer to the chapter on hearing and talking for more about this activity.)
- Digital pictures of the babies as they achieve each new skill (like rolling over) sent via e-mail or given to the parents
- E-mail messages sent to parents at work or home applauding a new skill that their baby has achieved
- A recorded phone message, changed daily or weekly, that summarizes any special events or reminders and that offers parents the opportunity to leave a message for the caregiver
- Bulletin boards and message notepads for parents to write down questions or comments for the caregivers
- Daily updates on a standard form, or in informal notes
- A monthly Saturday morning "Baby Play Day" only for dads and their babies
- Infant massage instructor who is invited to teach both caregivers and parents massage technique
- A "Fix-Up Day" that happens the first Saturday morning of every month. Parents are invited to the home or center to leave a book, picture, or toy for all the children to share, and to personalize any space that belongs to their child (for example, their child's crib area or cubby). This usually takes parents thirty minutes or less on a busy Saturday, but it has a long-lasting effect for both the child and the parents.
- Parents As Teachers (PAT) or similar parenting programs incorporated as valuable aspects of child care

Each baby in your care is unique. You may need to pay special attention to caring for some children with special needs. A child with a chaotic family background, or one from a cultural background different from yours, may take more of your attention. Many resources are available to help you in these areas—we mention some in the Resources section at the end of this book. You can also start your search for information in specific areas by contacting your local child care resource and referral agency.

Establishing Routines and Rituals

Babies' sense of security and trust in the world is directly related to their daily routines and rituals, which are provided by the consistent caregiver. Babies soon recognize that a voice or song is meant just for them and that it means something special—they are going to be rocked to sleep or played with or held. And how much more reassuring it would be if the same song their moms or dads sang to them at home was also the one they heard from their caregiver! Routines and rituals are great examples of the benefits of parents and the caregiver forming a partnership to reinforce a baby's security and trust. These repeated positive experiences speak to respecting the uniqueness of the individual child and reassuring the baby that, "I am okay, people love me, and I can depend on them to take care of me."

We recently viewed a video on infant massage. In it, we saw a foster grandparent who, from the time the baby was six weeks old, came a few times a week to the child care program to give a baby with special needs an infant massage. We viewed the reaction of the baby at three months old. As soon as the foster grandparent entered the room and greeted the baby, the baby showed signs of anticipation and delight. This is a good example of what we mean by security, trust, and predictability!

In your role as caregiver, take the time to set up routines and rituals for each baby in your care. Ask parents for their help—explain to them that their participation is very important. Routines and rituals change over the first fifteen months of a baby's life, so it is important that you talk with parents regularly. Some routines and rituals will be common for most of the babies in your care—like floor time to help increase their large-muscle development. But, as we have mentioned, most routines and rituals will be unique to the individual baby—special songs, the way each baby wants to be held, the time each baby wants to nap and be fed, and so on.

Security and trust are the foundation for the babies' sense of their own identity. Babies who have safe and predictable interactions will learn and develop—and, research tells us, most likely will do well in school as they get older. It is alarming that the highest turnover in child care staff is in the infant and toddler caregiving area. When a baby experiences four or five caregivers in one year, it is very likely that this little person has experienced repeated stress, anxiety, and unpredictability.

Supporting Each Baby's Developmental Journey

Babies can be very different from one another. One baby cries loudly. Another barely whimpers. Some babies kick and squirm. Others hardly move at all. Some babies are hypersensitive and fearful. Others are risk takers. As we know from brain research, each child's personality is developed through a mix of genetics (what children are born with— "nature") and environmental interaction (what they experience—"nurture"). As a caregiver, your goal, in partnership with the parents, is to nurture the babies' strengths and find ways to help them with their challenges. Simple activities that encourage coping and practicing skills early in babies' lives can help them learn and develop.

The activities in this book are grouped by natural, "brain-wired" areas where you will see regular growth as the baby matures:

- Vision
- Touch
- Language development
- Physical development
- Emotional and social development

Summary

This book explores each area of development that is key in the life of a baby. Each important area—sight, touch, sound, speech, movement, emotions, and social interaction— is covered in successive chapters. In addition to helpful information about each area, you will find many activities that you can do with babies to nurture their development. The activities involve minimal materials and outline simple directions to engage babies.

The services you provide as a caregiver are not only valuable but also critical to the growth of the babies in your care. The potential for learning and development, dramatically demonstrated during the first fifteen months of babies' lives, can be realized with the help of skilled caregivers. We hope this book will increase your understanding and ability to nurture babies' growth—because your work affects children's lifelong development.

Seeing: Activities

Chapter 1

Seeing: Activities That Nurture Babies' Development of Sight

The part of a baby's brain that controls sight begins to form by the time the baby is three months old. Vision is one of the slowest senses to develop. The world looks fuzzy to babies in the early months. They love faces and moving objects but don't develop full color vision until they are between four and seven months old. By age two, children still have not gained completely clear sight.

The American Academy of Pediatrics (AAP) recommends that infants have their sight tested by the age of six months, and have a formal vision screening by age three. This advice is particularly important if you notice older babies (beyond six months):

- Frequently crossing their eyes
- Shutting or covering one eye
- Holding objects very close to their eyes

Activities that give babies the chance to look at something interesting help them focus and improve their vision. During the first fifteen months of life, watching people and things around them is one of the most important ways babies begin exploring and understanding their world. The activities in this chapter can help babies develop their sight as well as thinking skills.

Faces, Faces, Faces

Materials

Lightweight cardboard (cardboard gift box, plain paper plate, etc.)
Marking pens
Scissors
Tape

Cut an 8- or 10-inch circle or oval shape from the cardboard. Use the marking pens to draw a face on the cardboard. Young babies will be most interested in the upper half of the face, so make sure the eyes and eyebrows are well defined.

What to Do with the Baby

- Tape the cardboard face to the side of the crib or to the wall within the baby's line of sight. Babies usually spend most of their time with their heads turned to their right.

- Talk to the baby about the face and the facial features: "This friendly face is happy to see you. Are those eyes looking at you? Is that face smiling at you?"

How This Helps the Baby

Young babies are attracted to shapes and patterns; they like to look at faces most of all. Of course, the best face to look at is the human face, so make sure you spend time with your own face close to the baby's when you are tending to or talking to him.

Fabric Whirl

Materials

Plastic lid from a margarine tub

3–4 different colored/patterned strips of washable fabric, cut 4–5 inches long and 2 inches wide (Use pinking shears to prevent the fabric from raveling.)

Scissors

Cloth tape

Needle and thread

Wash and dry the margarine lid. Carefully cut out the center of the lid, leaving a ring a half-inch wide. Cover the inside cut edge of the ring with cloth tape. Wrap the end of each fabric strip over the ring and sew it securely, leaving a 3- to 4-inch tail.

What to Do with the Baby

- Position the baby facing you, or hold the baby on your lap so you are facing each other.

- Spin the ring on your index finger. (The faster you spin it, the less control you have, so take care that the ring doesn't fly off your finger.)

- Describe what you are doing and what the baby is seeing—colors, movement, etc.: "I can spin the ring on my finger and make the colors go around and around."

- Place the ring on the baby's wrist, then gently spin the ring.

How This Helps the Baby

Colorful objects that move attract babies' attention. Very young babies are attracted to high-contrast colors such as black, white, and red. The Fabric Whirl encourages the baby to follow the movement with her eyes and perhaps to reach for it.

Visual Tracking

Materials

Rattle

What to Do with the Baby

- Position the baby on her back.
- Hold the rattle 8–10 inches above the baby's head.
- Shake the rattle to attract the baby's attention and get her to focus on it.
- Slowly move the rattle from one side of the baby's head to the other.
- Observe the baby's eyes to see if she follows the rattle. Does the baby move her head to keep the rattle in view?
- The baby may show enthusiasm for the game by moving arms and legs.
- Repeat the activity as long as the baby seems interested.

How This Helps the Baby

This activity encourages babies to focus and follow the rattle with both eyes.

Pinwheel

Materials

Pinwheel (purchased or home-made)

Safety Note: Pinwheels are not infant toys and should never be left in the crib or given to babies to play with on their own.

> **Hint:** Some gardening stores sell large, colorful pinwheels that are used to discourage birds from feasting on fruits and vegetables.

What to Do with the Baby

- Hold the pinwheel in your hand and position yourself so the baby can see you and the pinwheel.
- Blow on the pinwheel (or use your hand) to make the pinwheel spin.
- Make the pinwheel spin slowly and then quickly.
- Describe what you are doing and what the baby is seeing: "When I blow very hard, the pinwheel spins very fast."

How This Helps the Baby

This activity helps babies learn to focus their eyes on both near and far objects. Babies are particularly interested in things that move.

Funny Feet

Materials

Infant socks or booties
Felt pieces or fabric scraps
Needle and embroidery thread or yarn

Cut simple facial features (eyes, mouth, and nose) from the felt or fabric and sew them securely to the top side of each infant sock with thread or yarn.

Vary the activity by making Happy Hands. Instead of using socks or booties, sew the fabric facial features on the palms or back sides of infant mittens or gloves. You might cut off the fingers of the gloves to add even more interest to the activity.

What to Do with the Baby

- Put the booties on the baby's feet.

- Position the baby so the Funny Feet are in the baby's line of vision.

- Describe the Funny Feet to the baby, explaining the different colors in the "face" and the texture of the socks: "Your feet have very friendly faces. Can you see their big, blue eyes and their smiling faces? Do the Funny Feet feel warm and soft?"

- Encourage the baby to kick her legs and to use her hands to pat, pat, pat her own Funny Feet.

How This Helps the Baby

Putting the Funny Feet on babies for a few minutes each day encourages the discovery of hands and feet. This activity also encourages visual tracking as the babies focus on the movement of the "faces" on their feet or hands.

3-D Mobile

Materials

Molded plastic hanger
String or yarn
3–4 empty cardboard toilet-paper rolls
Scraps of patterned gift-wrapping paper (Choose bold patterns such as black-and-white stripes or checks.)
Tape or glue

Cut the string into 8- to 12-inch lengths. Cover the tubes with the wrapping paper and secure with tape or white glue. Tie one end of the string securely around the center of each tube, leaving a long tail. You can use a piece of tape to keep the string from shifting. Securely tie the loose ends of the strings to the hanger, spacing the tubes evenly.

Note: When designing your mobile, keep the baby's "point of view" in mind. The baby will usually be looking up at the mobile.

Vary this activity by hanging the mobile horizontally rather than vertically. Remember that babies find bold patterns much more interesting than cute, small pictures.

Safety Note: For safety's sake, be sure to remove mobiles from cribs or make sure they are well out of reach once the baby is able to sit up.

What to Do with the Baby

● Hang the mobile about 12-18 inches above the baby and slightly to the right side of the crib—the direction that young babies tend to look much of the time.

● Encourage the baby to focus on the mobile by gently tapping the tubes to make them move. Use your voice and facial expressions to reflect any interest or excitement shown by the baby: "You must like to look at this toy because you are smiling and kicking your feet."

● Make a variety of these mobiles and change them frequently to stimulate new interest.

How This Helps the Baby

This activity adds a different dimension to the baby's view from the crib and encourages eye focusing and movement. Babies are attracted to the shape, colorful design, and movement of the tubes. Older babies will begin to associate the words you use to describe the mobile with a particular action or object.

Ribbon Flutter

Materials

Brightly colored ribbons (leftover from birthdays or other celebrations)

Cut the ribbons to lengths of not more than 12 inches. Tie a bundle of 4–6 of the ribbons together at one end with more ribbon. Babies love to watch the ribbons move, so hang them where they will flutter in a breeze—attached to a curtain rod, perhaps. The ribbons can also be suspended over a crib or changing table but must be positioned so the baby cannot reach them when she is sitting.

What to Do with the Baby

● Describe what the baby is seeing (different colors, movement, etc.): "The bright red ribbons are dancing just for you."

● Place the baby in new positions (or carry her in your arms) so she can see the ribbons from different angles.

● Encourage older babies to run and dance with the ribbons.

How This Helps the Baby

The Ribbon Flutter gives babies the opportunity to practice focusing and following movement with their eyes.

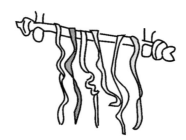

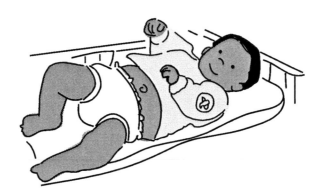

Spoon Pal

Materials

Wooden spoon
Indelible markers
6-inch piece of ribbon (optional)

Check the wooden spoon for rough spots and sand it if necessary. Wash the spoon in hot, soapy water and dry it thoroughly. Use the markers to draw a face on the bowl of the spoon. If you want, you can draw a face on each side of the spoon—maybe a happy face on one side and a sad face on the other. Tie the ribbon around the spoon handle just below the bowl.

Safety Note: It is best to purchase a new spoon for this activity to be certain that it is free of any cooking residue. Also, be sure the markers you use to decorate the spoon are nontoxic and indelible because the spoon is sure to end up in the baby's mouth on occasion.

What to Do with the Baby

- Hold the baby in your lap.
- Show the baby the Spoon Pal, moving it in different ways so it will seem to dance or jump.
- Encourage the baby to grasp the Spoon Pal in his own hands.
- Talk about the Spoon Pal. Describe the colors you used to draw the face, the soft ribbon, and the texture of the wood: "Your Spoon Pal has a very sad face. Let's make that sad face into a happy face. There is its happy face!"

How This Helps the Baby

Babies are attracted to the shape and facial features of this Spoon Pal. The toy helps younger babies focus their eyes and older babies improve eye-hand coordination.

Picture Gallery

Materials

3–5 plastic lids from margarine tubs

3–5 pieces of printed fabric, patterned wallpaper, magazine pictures, greeting cards, etc.,
   that are cut to fit inside the lids

Glue

Tape (optional)

Clear Con-Tact paper (optional)

Wash and dry the lids. Glue one of the picture/pattern shapes you cut inside each lid and let the glue dry thoroughly. Covering the pictures with clear Con-Tact paper makes them more durable.

You can vary the activity by giving several of the pictures to the baby to manipulate on her own instead of hanging the pictures on the wall.

What to Do with the Baby

- Tape the lids to the wall next to the baby's crib or changing table, or on the wall in a play area. Young babies tend to look to the right more often than to the left.

- Point to the pictures and talk to the baby about the different pictures. Describe the colors and designs: "There is a big, brown bear on your wall. The bear is looking at you."

How This Helps the Baby

These simple pictures help babies focus and encourage them to use their eyes to search and then position their heads and bodies so they can observe what they want.

Bubbles

Materials

Bubble solution (Make your own by mixing a generous squirt of dishwashing detergent with a quart of water, or use purchased bubble solution.)
Bubble wand (Make your own using a piece of flexible wire.)

Safety Note: Make sure the bubbles you blow float away from young babies so the bubbles don't pop on their faces.

What to Do with the Baby

- Place the baby so she can watch you.
- Blow bubbles so the baby can watch them as they float away.
- Talk to the baby about the bubbles: "The bubbles float in the air and pop!"
- Older babies will enjoy chasing and trying to catch the bubbles.

How This Helps the Baby

Bubbles are slow moving, and babies can follow them with their eyes. This is a great outdoor activity on a breezy day. Children of all ages enjoy bubbles; it's nearly impossible to blow bubbles or watch them without laughing and smiling.

Rainbow Sun-Catcher

Materials

3–4 clear plastic lids from yogurt containers
3–4 colored highlighter marking pens
Sharp scissors or hole punch
8-inch piece of string or yarn for each lid

Wash and dry the lids. Use a highlighter marking pen to color the top surface of one of the lids. Let the ink dry, then punch a small hole near the edge of the lid. Push the end of the string through the hole and tie a knot so the lid dangles. Repeat this process using a different colored highlighter marking pen for each lid. Securely attach the loose ends of the strings to a curtain rod so the lids catch the sunlight. Make sure the baby cannot reach the lids.

What to Do with the Baby

- Hold or position the baby so he can see the colorful lids.
- Say the name of the color as you point to each lid: "The blue light is bouncing around the room."
- Gently tap the lids so they swing in the sunlight.
- Repeat this activity at different times of the day so the baby can observe how the lids appear in dim and bright sunlight.

How This Helps the Baby

The bold colors and movement of the lids help babies develop their ability to focus on and follow objects with their eyes.

Mirror, Mirror on the Wall

Materials

Long, narrow mirror
Handrail, and hardware to install handrail

Along one wall of your baby's room, approximately 1 inch above the floor, secure a long, narrow mirror (or several smaller mirrors) horizontally. (Mirrors made with safety glass or other safe reflective materials are often sold through early-childhood catalogs.) Attach the handrail just above the mirror. Make sure the rail is secured to the wall studs and that the rail is no more than 2⅜ inches out from the wall.

What to Do with the Baby

- During the baby's floor time, place the baby on her side or tummy in front of the mirror and encourage her to look at herself in the mirror. Babies will coo and smile at their own reflections.
- Older babies will enjoy watching themselves roll over, rock, and crawl.
- The baby will eventually use the secured handrail above the mirror to pull up to a standing position.

How This Helps the Baby

The low mirror provides the baby with a different view of the environment. The movement and reflections in the mirror encourage babies to focus their eyes and to move their heads and bodies. The low handrail offers a safe place to practice pulling up to a standing position as babies prepare to take their first steps.

Peek-a-Boo Mirror

Materials

Heavy cardboard
Sturdy scissors (or sharp utility knife)
Mirror, no larger than the cardboard
Strapping tape
Con-Tact paper
Fabric
Measuring tape or ruler
Pencil
Stickers and marking pens (optional)

Cut a 1-foot-square piece of heavy cardboard. Measure the length and width of the mirror. Subtract ½ inch from each measurement. Cut a rectangle the size of this measurement from the center of the cardboard. "Frame" the mirror by securely taping it to the back of the cardboard so the mirrored side shows through the frame. Cover the back of the mirror and cardboard with Con-Tact paper to make sure the mirror stays put. Decorate the frame with stickers or markers, if you choose. Then, cut a 1-foot square from the fabric. Using the strapping tape, create a flap by attaching the fabric square to the top of the front of the frame, covering the mirror. Now, securely attach the Peek-a-Boo Mirror to the wall or divider at the baby's eye level.

What to Do with the Baby

● Position the baby to face the fabric-covered mirror.

● Raise the fabric flap and say, "Peek-a-boo!"

● Lower the fabric flap.

● Repeat.

● Help the baby raise the fabric flap. Say, "Peek-a-boo!"

● Repeat, repeat, repeat.

How This Helps the Baby

Babies enjoy watching their own faces (and yours) appear and disappear. This activity encourages babies to focus their eyes and helps them begin to understand that something can exist even if they cannot see it.

Discovering the Outdoors

Materials

Stroller or baby buggy

Safety Note: Make sure the baby is dressed appropriately for the weather.

What to Do with the Baby

- Rather than just pushing the stroller on your regular outdoor walks, hesitate for a few minutes in areas where the baby can watch the shadows, tree patterns, clouds, birds, water, and other movement and colors.

- Talk to the baby about the surroundings. Describe the colors and the movement: "The sky is so blue this morning. Do you see those puffy, white clouds up in the sky?"

How This Helps the Baby

Babies need to spend time outdoors—it is just as much a part of their visual environment as the inside of your home or center. The baby and you will enjoy discovering new and interesting things to watch—especially if you live where there are distinct seasonal changes.

Acceleration

Materials

Ball or toys with wheels
Sturdy cardboard
Pillows or books

Prop the cardboard on the pillows or books to make a ramp to the floor.
Vary this activity by using an empty paper-towel tube. Let the wheeled objects roll through the tube onto the floor.

What to Do with the Baby

- Hold a toy or a ball at the top of the cardboard ramp and let go of it.
- Observe as the baby watches the object roll down the ramp.
- Repeat.
- Change the level of the ramp to control how fast the object rolls down.
- Describe what the baby is observing: "The car is moving very fast."
- Help the baby place the object at the top of the ramp and encourage him to let go so the object races down.
- Roll the object up the ramp and let it roll back down. Help the baby repeat this movement.

How This Helps the Baby

This activity helps babies develop their visual tracking and eye-hand coordination. It gives babies firsthand experience with the properties of gravity.

Flashlight Fun

Materials

Flashlight

What to Do with the Baby

- Turn out the lights or close the blinds to slightly darken the room.
- Turn on the flashlight and shine the light around the room.
- Pause to name the objects you catch in the beam of light: "Look, I see your teddy bear sitting in the chair."
- Older babies will enjoy holding the flashlight themselves and making the light move around the room.

How This Helps the Baby

This activity supports the development of babies' visual tracking ability as their eyes follow the movement of the light.

Touching: Activities

Chapter 2

Touching: Activities That Develop Babies' Sense of Touch

The effect of infant massage on a baby attests to the early impact of the human touch in a child's development. A recent study by the Touch Research Institute at the University of Miami showed that premature babies who had daily massages gained weight 47 percent faster than those who did not have massages. Babies who received the massages had fewer signs of anxiety and stress. We know that nurturing a baby's sense of touch is linked to both mental and physical development in children.

Babies respond to human touch but also to the feel of things. Newborns can distinguish between soft and coarse materials next to their bodies. Experienced parents and caregivers know that some babies are more sensitive to touch than others. One four-month-old baby cried unexplainably when her parents took her to a caregiver. The caregiver tried everything to console the baby but to no avail. The caregiver finally enlisted the help of the parents, and they went through a checklist of possibilities. The mother suspected that it just might be that the baby was missing the silky blanket that she had at home in her crib. Sure enough!

The activities in this chapter can help babies develop their sense of touch.

Fuzzy Bottle

Materials

Baby bottle
Fuzzy sock

When you are ready to feed the baby, slip the baby's bottle into a fuzzy sock. Use a sock that fits the bottle yet does not cover up the bottle cap and nipple.

What to Do with the Baby

- Hold and cuddle the baby while you feed him.
- Talk to the baby about the texture the baby is touching: "Your bottle feels very soft this morning."

How This Helps the Baby

Babies are experiencing the world with their senses; they are very sensitive to touch. The fuzzy bottle will give a baby something different to touch as you feed him.

Texture Poke Box

Materials

Shallow box with removable lid (1½–2 inches deep)
4–6 pieces of material, each with a different texture
 (scraps of fake fur, corduroy, terry cloth, velvet, ridged
 cardboard or paper, burlap, satin, soft nylon netting, felt,
 textured wallpaper, etc.)
Pencil or pen
Ruler
White glue
Cloth tape
Scissors or craft knife
Cotton balls (optional)

> **Hint:** Place a few cotton balls underneath one or two of the sections of textured material before gluing in place to make them a little puffy.

With a pencil and the aid of a ruler, draw dividing lines on the inside of the bottom of the box and the top of the lid to create 4–6 equal sections. The bottom and the lid should have the same number of sections; the size and basic shape of the box will determine the number and shape of the sections. Cut a different piece of textured material to fit each section in the bottom of the box, and glue securely in place.

Find and mark the center of each section of the lid. Use scissors or a craft knife to cut out a small circle about the size of a quarter from the center of each section. Cover the cut edge of each circle with cloth tape to make it smooth and more durable.

Place the lid on the box and tape the box closed on all four sides.

What to Do with the Baby

- Hold the baby on your lap.
- Poke your finger into one of the holes in the lid of the box and describe what you are doing and what you feel with your finger: "My finger feels something bumpy."
- Gently help the baby poke one of his own fingers into the same hole. Describe the texture the baby is feeling: "Now *your* finger feels something bumpy."
- Repeat with the other finger holes.

How This Helps the Baby

Babies are very sensitive to touch, so they enjoy exploring with their fingers. The texture box holds babies' attention and allows you to repeat words that describe what they are touching. This sensory activity also creates a wonderful opportunity for helping the babies begin to learn about categorization—comparing the feel of one texture to another.

Exploring the Outdoors

Materials

Stroller or baby buggy

Safety Note: Make sure the baby is dressed appropriately for the weather.

What to Do with the Baby

- On your regular outdoor walks, stop along the way to let the baby feel a smooth, round boulder, coarse bark of a tree trunk, prickly pine needles, soft grass, cool water, etc.

- Describe what the baby is feeling and seeing: "The water is cool and wet."

How This Helps the Baby

Babies like to touch, poke, squeeze, rub, and pat interesting objects. This activity gives them the opportunity to experience a variety of textures that are usually only found outside.

Hungry Caterpillar and Other Feely Friends

Materials

5–6 carpet pieces, each with a different color and texture
Heavy scissors or utility knife
Carpet tape

Use scissors or a utility knife to cut each carpet piece into a circle (or appropriate shapes for another feely friend, such as a ladybug or a butterfly). At the baby's eye level, secure the carpet circles to the wall with the carpet tape, placing them in an undulating row to form the caterpillar shape.

What to Do with the Baby

- Position the baby so she can touch the different textures on the carpet pieces.
- Talk to the baby about the textures she is feeling. Use descriptive words such as *soft, nubby, fluffy, smooth*, etc.
- Extend this activity by reading *The Very Hungry Caterpillar* by Eric Carle.

How This Helps the Baby

Babies love to see and feel these carpet characters. This activity is also a wonderful way to help babies make the connection between the language you use to describe a variety of textures and what they are touching.

Texture Book

Materials

8 fabric pieces, each with a different texture (corduroy, satin, burlap, flannel, terry cloth, wool, polished cotton, silk, lace, etc.)
Scissors
Needle and thread

Cut each piece of fabric into a 6- or 8-inch square. Stack the fabric squares and sew them together on one edge so they look like a book.

What to Do with the Baby

- Hold the baby on your lap so he can touch the fabric book.
- Touch the first fabric square and describe how it feels to you (smooth, rough, bumpy, soft): "This piece of cloth feels slippery and soft."
- Invite the baby to touch the fabric square. Help the very young baby touch the fabric or rub the fabric square against his hand, cheek, or leg.
- Repeat with the remaining fabric squares.
- Extend this activity by describing the colors and patterns of each fabric square.

How This Helps the Baby

This activity gives babies a lot of different things they can touch, or have touch them, which helps babies become aware of a variety of textures and learn to distinguish between them.

Float and Sink

Materials

Dishpan of room-temperature water
Objects that float (sponge, rubber duck, etc.)
Objects that sink (spoon, large smooth stone, etc.)
Towels

What to Do with the Baby

- Place the pan of water on a floor or table protected with towels.

- Sit with the baby where she can reach the water.

- Place an object that will float in the pan of water. Push the object under the water and let go so it will pop back above the water. Let the baby try.

- Talk to the baby about what she is seeing and doing: "The duck floats on the water. When you push the duck under the water, it pops back up."

- Repeat with the objects that sink: "The spoon goes plop and falls to the bottom."

How This Helps the Baby

Water is very interesting to babies because of the way it feels and moves.

Touchy Drop Box

Materials

Empty cube-shaped tissue box
5 lids from baby-food jars
5 pieces of material, each with a different texture (satin, nubby wallpaper, fake fur, terry
   cloth, felt, etc.)
Cloth tape or strapping tape
Ruler
Scissors or pinking shears
Glue

Remove the plastic-film insert from the opening in the top of the tissue box. Cover the
   edge of the opening with cloth tape or strapping tape. Measure one side of the tissue
   box and cut four pieces of the material, each with a different texture, to fit. Measure the
   bottom of the tissue box and cut the remaining piece of material to fit. (Use pinking
   shears to make the edges attractive and to prevent the fabric from raveling.) Glue the
   fabric pieces to the sides and the bottom of the tissue box; let the glue dry thoroughly.
   Using the same five fabrics, trace the outline of a jar lid on each of the five different
   pieces of fabric. Cut out the circles and glue them to the insides or outsides of the jar
   lids. Let the glue dry thoroughly.

What to Do with the Baby

- Sit on the floor with the baby.
- Place all of the jar lids inside the texture box and shake it to attract the
  baby's attention.
- Let the baby hold the box while you describe the different textures he is feeling: "That
  feels rough and bumpy."
- Dump the jar lids out of the box and let the baby explore the textures.
- Help the baby drop the lids through the opening at the top of the texture box.

How This Helps the Baby

Young babies enjoy exploring the different textures on the outside of the box and on the
jar lids. Older babies will still enjoy the textures on the box, but they will be more interested in dropping the jar lids inside and then dumping them out.

Sticky Feet

Materials

Con-Tact paper
Masking or strapping tape
Carpet (optional)

Cut a 1-foot-square piece of Con-Tact paper and tape it, sticky side up, to a clean floor
   or a piece of carpet. Masking tape or strapping tape does a good job of holding the
   Con-Tact paper in place.

What to Do with the Baby

- Remove the baby's shoes and socks.

- Stand the baby on the sticky surface.

- Encourage him to walk on the sticky surface.

- Talk to the baby about what he is feeling: "Your feet want to stick to the floor."
  "Your feet make a funny sound when you walk on the sticky floor."

- Allow the baby to explore the area on his own. The baby may want to experiment
  by touching the sticky surface or placing a toy on
  the surface.

- Throughout the day, remember to say the
  word "sticky" to describe other appropriate
  situations: "Your hands are sticky after
  eating the piece of banana."

- If the baby is not interested in the
  sticky surface, leave it in place for
  a while and observe how he
  avoids stepping on it.

How This Helps the Baby

This activity increases babies'
awareness of touch sensations.
It also helps them to learn what
sticky feels like and to distinguish
that feeling from others.

Frosty Fun

Materials

Water
Ice-cube tray
High chair with a tray, or a rimmed cookie sheet
Paper towels

Fill the ice-cube tray with clean water and freeze overnight.

What to Do with the Baby

- While holding the baby in your arms, remove the ice-cube tray from the freezer. Say, "This is cold."
- Place the baby in the high chair and secure the strap, or on a chair at a low table.
- Place one ice cube on the high-chair tray or on the cookie sheet at the table.
- Observe what the baby does with the ice cube. The baby may touch it, pick it up, or just look at it.
- Describe what the baby is seeing and touching: "You are touching ice. It is very cold."
- As the ice melts, describe what is happening: "The ice is getting smaller as it turns back into water."
- Use the paper towel to absorb the water, and let the baby touch it.
- Extend this activity by finding other cold things for the baby to touch, and by reading books about ice and snow.

How This Helps the Baby

This activity lets the baby explore hot and cold sensations through touch and build awareness of touch both in temperature (how *hot* and *cold* feel) and firmness (hard ice cube and soft paper towel).

Hearing and Talking: Activities

Chapter 3

Hearing and Talking: Activities That Encourage Babies' Language Development

At birth, newborns can usually distinguish their mothers' voices from "listening" to them while in utero. Newborns can distinguish loud from quiet sounds, but tend to tune in much more to the high-pitched coos from adults. By four to six months, babies can track the sources of the sounds around them. Hearing is the critical link to a baby's language acquisition and speech development. The American Academy of Pediatrics (AAP) recommends screening for hearing loss before the baby is three months old. This screening is especially important if you notice that a baby is consistently not turning his head or eyes toward the source of a sound (for example, a musical toy or a vacuum cleaner) by the time the baby is six months old. A temporary hearing loss can happen when a baby has a bad cold or allergy and the baby's ear canals are blocked. If this happens frequently to a baby in your care, encourage the parents to work with their doctor to find a solution.

Part of your concern as a caregiver is to be sure that the baby can hear properly, and the other part of the concern is what and how often the baby hears sounds and language. All babies have their own timetables for expressive language (talking), but receptive language (what a baby hears) builds from infancy. Reading to babies from the time they are newborns, talking to them in different intonations, singing to them, and repeating rhymes and jingles are all steps to language and speech development.

It is important to remember that a baby does not learn and distinguish language from just hearing tapes of music or books or conversations. The baby needs to see your face and lips when you speak and pronounce the sounds of words. So, when you are talking with a baby, look at him and, when he makes a sound, repeat it. Talk to the baby about things you are doing together—whether it is changing a diaper or getting the baby ready to go outdoors. The baby will respond with smiles, babbles, and coos. From about eight to eighteen months, those babbled words become babbled sentences with one or two clear and recognizable words—which you repeat back to the baby and applaud!

Especially in the early months of life, crying is a big part of the baby's "language." As you observe and understand each of the babies in your care, you will become more conscious of their distinct crying language. You will hear the difference between pain, hunger, discomfort, fear, or exhaustion in their cries. The crying language gets more complex as the baby becomes older, and more emotions—like frustration—become evident. Whatever the age, think of crying as a way the baby is talking to you. Pay attention and respond to the baby with reassurance or with whatever you think may be the best response.

Because hearing, speech, and language are so closely intertwined, we are considering them together in the activities created for this chapter.

The Baby Beat Goes On

Materials

Empty cylindrical oatmeal box with lid (Clean plastic food containers and empty coffee cans also make instant drums.)
Wooden kitchen spoon (optional)

What to Do with the Baby

- Set the "drum" in front of the baby.
- Tap on the top of the drum, using your whole hand for a loud beat or just your fingers for a gentler beat.
- Tap out simple rhythmic patterns, for example: *tap* (pause) *tap-tap*; or *tap-tap-tap* (pause) *tap*.
- Tap on the side of the drum to create a different tone.
- Talk about your actions and what the baby is hearing: "Boom, boom, boom goes the drum when I strike it with my hand."
- Help the baby use her own hand(s) to tap out her own tune. Don't expect the baby to tap rhythmically.
- Use a wooden spoon to beat the drum to renew interest or to add a level of difficulty to the baby's own drumming experience.

How This Helps the Baby

Babies are interested in both familiar and unfamiliar sounds. These activities help babies develop listening skills and encourage them to become aware of rhythms and patterns. Beating the drum also helps babies develop eye-hand coordination.

Say Again

Materials

None

What to Do with the Baby

- Position the baby so you are facing each other and can make eye contact.
- Use your normal tone of voice and make a repetitive sound such as "da, da, da" or "la, la, la."
- Observe the baby's response.
- If there is no response from the baby, repeat the sound again.
- If the baby makes a sound, mimic it.
- Observe the baby's response.
- Encourage communication by enthusiastically mimicking all of the baby's attempts at vocalization.

How This Helps the Baby

Babies learn about language by imitating sounds around them. This activity encourages babies to experiment with the different sounds they can make with their own voices. It also helps them to begin to learn about the give-and-take involved in using language to communicate—listening and talking.

Lullabies and Music

Materials

Musical recordings and/or instruments (CDs/tapes, a music box, radio, piano, or other instruments)

What to Do with the Baby

- Sing lullabies that are traditional, inserting the baby's name when appropriate.
- Turn on a radio or music box. Note that babies startle at loud, harsh-sounding music but are soothed by background, classical, or rhythmic music.
- Play a music CD or tape.
- Play a few chords on a piano, guitar, or other instrument.

How This Helps the Baby

As a newborn, the baby can hear the sound and rhythm of music whether it is played or sung. These early experiences with music help the baby hear the melody, rhythm, and flow of language. By the time babies are about twelve months old, you will see them clap their hands and bounce to the beat.

Read to Me

Materials

Cloth books
Soft-vinyl books
Heavy cardboard books
Other books

What to Do with the Baby

- From cloth or soft-vinyl books, read the simple words and describe the image on each page. Allow the baby to hold, touch, and mouth the book.
- Let older babies (six to fifteen months) drag heavy-cardboard books around so they can enjoy turning the pages and looking at the pictures whenever they wish.
- From other books, occasionally read a short story or nursery rhyme to the baby.

How This Helps the Baby

Babies can learn to feel comfortable with books and enjoy them at an early age. This enjoyment will serve to motivate and help them read and write later on.

There are some beautiful and melodic poems, nursery rhymes, and short stories from many different cultures that are now in children's literature books. You may know some of your favorites from memory. Here are some nursery rhymes and books to get you started.

Nursery Rhymes

Pat-a-cake, pat-a-cake
Baker's man.
Bake me a cake
As fast as you can.
Roll it and pat it
And mark it with a "B."
Put it in the oven
For baby and me.

Humpty Dumpty sat on a wall.
Humpty Dumpty had a great fall.
All the king's horses
And all the king's men
Couldn't put Humpty
Together again.

Rock-a-bye Baby
In the tree top.
When the wind blows,
The cradle will rock.
When the bough breaks,
The cradle will fall,
And down will come baby,
Cradle and all.

Books

Animals in the Zoo. Feodor Rojankovsky, New York: Knopf, 1962.
Baby's Catalogue. Janet and Allan Ahlberg, Boston: Little, Brown, 1982.
Goodnight Moon. Margaret Wise Brown, New York: Harper Collins, 1991, 1947.
Hand Rhymes. Marc Tolon Brown, Great Britain: Collins, Picture Lions, 1987.
The Helen Oxenbury Nursery Rhyme Book (rhymes chosen by Brian Alderson). New York: Morrow, 1987.
More, More, More Said the Baby. Vera B. Williams, New York: Greenwillow Books, 1990.
Pat the Bunny. Dorothy Kunhardt, Racine, Wisconsin: Western Publishing Company, 1997.
The Real Mother Goose. Blanche Fisher Wright, New York: Checkerboard, 1987, 1944.
Tickle, Tickle. Helen Oxenbury, New York: Little Simon, 1999.
The Very Hungry Caterpillar. Eric Carle, New York: Philomel Books, 1994, 1969.
What Is It? Tana Hoban, New York: Greenwillow Books, 1985.

Sandwich-Bag Book

Materials

6–8 resealable plastic sandwich bags

6–8 flat objects (felt shapes, photographs, thin sponges, artificial leaves, silk flowers, paper or crocheted doilies, short lengths of ribbon, plastic lids, etc.)

Cloth tape or strapping tape

Be creative when choosing the flat objects for the book, but make sure they are safe for the baby.

Seal one flat object inside each plastic sandwich bag. Stack the filled bags and tape them all together on the resealable side with colorful cloth tape or strapping tape to form a book shape.

What to Do with the Baby

- Make reading a part of your daily routine.
- Hold the baby in your lap and cuddle while you explore this unusual book.
- Describe what the baby is observing on each page of the book: "This flower is a daisy. It has a bright, yellow center."
- Encourage and/or help the baby to touch the objects. Even through the plastic, these objects will still have depth and texture.

How This Helps the Baby

Reading to babies for even the few minutes it takes to "read" this book (or other simple books) is a powerful way to build literacy skills in young children. This book is durable and will stand up to repeated usage by the baby.

Greeting Card Book

Materials

Greeting cards
Paper punch
Shoelace (no more than 12 inches in length)

Choose greeting cards with simple, colorful pictures. Using only the fronts of the cards, trim six to eight of them so they are the same size. Punch three evenly spaced holes in the edge of one card. This card can now be used as a guide to punch matching holes in the remaining cards. Stack the cards so the holes line up, and "sew" them together with the shoelace. Tie a knot or a bow with any excess shoelace.

Vary the activity by making several greeting card books with different themes using holiday greeting cards or cards with pictures of animals, birds, flowers, or whatever else you can think of—the possibilities are endless.

What to Do with the Baby

- Make reading a part of your daily routine.
- Hold the baby on your lap and cuddle while you read the book.
- Talk to the baby about the different pictures in the book and what they represent: "The pretty yellow bird is smelling the blue flower."
- Encourage the baby to explore this book with hands and fingers. (Many greeting cards are embossed, which gives them an interesting texture.)
- Connect the book to real-life experiences. If a card has a picture of a tree or a flower, show the baby a real-life example of a tree or a flower. Let the baby touch, smell, and otherwise experience the real thing.

How This Helps the Baby

Babies pay attention longer when themes are varied. You can customize the book using themes that interest babies (animals, birds, colors, etc.) and will hold their attention as you read the book together. This activity helps babies develop language skills and offers them the chance to mimic others in their lives who read.

Paper-Plate Book

Materials

4 thin paper plates
Yarn
4 colorful magazine pictures of faces, animals, etc.
Paper punch
Glue

Trim the magazine pictures to fit the centers of the paper plates, then glue the pictures in place. Using the paper punch, make two or three evenly spaced holes on the left or top edge of one of the paper plates. Use this plate as a guide to punch holes in the remaining paper plates. Stack the plates and loosely tie a separate short loop of yarn through each set of holes. Keep the yarn loose so the pages of this paper-plate book will turn easily.

Vary the activity by drawing your own pictures—a happy face, house, dog, tree—using crayons or markers.

> **Hint:** Ask the babies' parents to provide you with magazine pictures. This makes it more likely that they will be culturally familiar to the baby.

What to Do with the Baby

● Make reading a part of your daily routine.

● Hold the baby on your lap and cuddle while you read together.

● Use expressive language to describe the pictures in the book: "The bird in the picture has beautiful red feathers."

● If you are bilingual, use words from both languages to describe the pictures.

How This Helps the Baby

This book is durable and encourages babies to handle it. The stiff paper plates are easy for babies to grasp so they can help you turn the pages as you read the book together. This activity helps babies develop listening skills and language.

Paper-Plate Puppet

Materials

2 paper plates
Crayons or marking pens
Scissors
Tape

Use the crayons or markers to draw a face on the bottom of one of the paper plates. Cut the other paper plate in half. Place the whole plate and the half-plate together so the fronts are facing each other and the rims are lined up evenly. Tape the two plates together around the rim.

What to Do with the Baby

- Slip your hand into the pocket that was formed when the two plates were taped together.
- Use a silly voice to make the puppet talk or sing to the baby.
- Include the baby in conversations you have with the puppet.
- Older babies will enjoy taking directions from the puppet.

How This Helps the Baby

Puppets can be used to extend many language activities. The use of puppets encourages babies to pay attention to what you are saying, which in turn helps them develop their listening skills and expand their vocabulary.

Who's That Baby in the Mirror?

Materials

Large mirror

What to Do with the Baby

- Sit with the baby in front of the mirror. If you sit on the floor, you can prop the baby between your outstretched legs.
- Clap your hands and kick your feet. Gently help the baby do the same.
- Talk to the baby about the things you are both seeing in the reflection. Cheer the baby on: "Erin is clap, clap, clapping her hands."
- Observe the baby's reactions and repeat movements that attract the baby's attention.

How This Helps the Baby

This activity helps support early language development by helping the baby associate actions with words.

Rhythm and Rhyme

Materials

None

What to Do with the Baby

- Place the baby on your lap so he is facing you.
- Hold the baby's hands in yours.
- Say or sing a nursery rhyme or song while you use the baby's hands to make the motions. "Row, Row, Row Your Boat," "Pat-a-Cake," and "The Itsy-Bitsy Spider" are perfect for this activity.
- Do this several times so the baby begins to anticipate what is coming next.

How This Helps the Baby

These songs and rhymes may be very familiar to you, but to babies they are brand new and delightful. This activity lets babies experience the rhythm of language. They may try to imitate you and experiment with using their voices in different ways.

Finger Puppet

Materials

Ball-point pen (not indelible ink)
Index-finger portion of a white cotton or rubber glove (optional)

Use the pen to draw a simple face on the tip of your index finger. Draw eyes and a smiling face. If you wish, cut the index finger from a white cotton glove or rubber glove and draw the face on the tip.

What to Do with the Baby

- Hold the baby on your lap, or place her on her back on the floor or in the crib.
- Hold your finger so the baby can focus on it.
- Introduce the finger puppet to the baby: "Look who came to play with you today. She has a big smile just for you."
- Use the finger puppet to name the different parts of the baby's body. The puppet can "tap your knee, hide under your chin, tickle your feet, look in your ear," and so on.
- Talk with the finger puppet about what you are doing: "You liked to tickle Toby's feet. You want to do it again?"

How This Helps the Baby

The finger puppet helps the baby focus on your words as you name the different parts of the baby's body.

Indoor Field Trip

Materials

Everyday objects located in the home or child care environment

What to Do with the Baby

- Hold the baby in your arms, positioning him so both of you see the same things.
- Slowly walk around and point out different objects in the room.
- Name and describe several objects in a section of the room and then move on to another area.
- Name and describe objects such as a chair, window, lamp, plant, refrigerator, stove, table, bed, telephone, clock, rug, light switch, ceiling fan, door, or door knob.
- Demonstrate how the object is used: "Troy and I can sit in the chair." "The lamp has a switch that turns the light on and off. See, the light goes on and off."
- Observe the baby's reactions to what you are saying and what the baby is seeing.
- With an older baby, repeat the name of the object several times and encourage the baby to make the same sounds you are making. Let your voice reflect the tone and mood of the baby's response.
- Exaggerate the different sounds of the letters in the names of the objects.

How This Helps the Baby

Babies listen to the caregiver's voice and become familiar with the sounds they make with their own mouths, lips, and throats. This activity invites babies to experiment with different sounds and encourages them to begin making the connection between concrete objects and words.

Sandwich Book

Materials

6 resealable plastic sandwich bags
Craft felt (brown, green, red, yellow, and pink)
Scissors
Cloth tape or strapping tape

Cut the brown felt into "bread slices" that will fit into the sandwich bags. Be creative in making the sandwich "fillings": a ruffle of lettuce from the green felt, a circle or two of red tomatoes, a square of yellow cheese, a square or round slice of pink ham, an oval green pickle or two. Place one sandwich filling in each of the bags. Seal each bag and stack them (resealable edges together) in the order you wish to build your sandwich—slice of bread, lettuce, tomato, cheese, ham, pickle, and another slice of bread. Tape the bags together with colorful cloth tape or strapping tape to form a book.

What to Do with the Baby

- Make reading a part of your daily routine.
- Hold the baby on your lap.
- Use descriptive words to tell a story about the sandwich: "The bread is brown and soft; the lettuce is green and crispy. Yum!"

How This Helps the Baby

Babies find the different colors and shapes of the sandwich fillings to be visually stimulating. They begin connecting food items and words. Older babies enjoy sound effects and learn to associate those sounds with certain foods.

Hide-and-Peek Box

Materials

Box with lid
One of the baby's favorite toys that will fit completely in the box

What to Do with the Baby

- While the baby is watching, say, "Bye-bye, rabbit." Then place the toy inside the box and replace the lid.

- Say, "Where is the rabbit?" Or ask, "Can you take the rabbit out of the box?"

- If necessary, help the baby discover where the toy is hiding. Act surprised and delighted to discover it.

- Repeat as many times as the baby seems attentive. To renew interest in this activity, add a second box. Hide a toy in only one box, adding an element of mystery: "Which box is the toy in?"

How This Helps the Baby

This activity supports the development of the babies' listening skills. They are developing the ability to hold a mental image of the toy and to understand that the toy, even though out of sight, has not gone away. This is called *object permanence*.

Copycat

Materials

None

What to Do with the Baby

- Sit on the floor with the baby so you are facing each other.
- Make gestures and sounds for the baby to imitate. (Pat the top of your head, stick out your tongue, blink your eyes, pat your tummy, clap your hands, open and close your hands, wave hello, shake your head yes and no, etc.)
- Talk to the baby about the actions: "I'm patting the top of my head. Can you pat the top of your head? Now we are both patting the tops of our heads."

How This Helps the Baby

This activity encourages the baby to listen to your voice and associate words with the actions you perform.

Baby Face

Materials

Magazine pictures of faces (Parenting magazines often have large, full-face pictures of babies, toddlers, and adults.)

What to Do with the Baby

- Hold a magazine picture so the baby can see it and you.
- Point to an eye and say, "Eye."
- Gently touch the baby's eye and say, "Eye."
- Point to your own eye and again say, "Eye."
- Ask the baby to find an eye in the picture, then your eye and the baby's own eye.
- Repeat this procedure for the nose, ears, and mouth.
- Depending on the baby, you may want to concentrate on only one facial feature for a couple of days. Stress the particular facial feature several times throughout each day by pointing out the eyes and other features of stuffed animals, dolls, or pictures of animals.

How This Helps the Baby

This activity helps babies expand their listening ability while building their awareness of the different parts of the face and the names of those parts.

Telephone

Materials

2 toy telephones
Tape recorder and blank tape

What to Do with the Baby

- Put one toy telephone in front of you and one in front of the baby.
- Pretend you are calling the baby on the phone: "Hello, Annie. What are you going to do today?" The baby will imitate you quite quickly by picking up the phone and babbling.
- Increase the number of your short, simple phrases and questions as the baby begins to respond.
- On the blank tape, record a conversation between the baby and you, and then play it back so the baby can listen to it.

How This Helps the Baby

This activity helps babies to learn words and phrases and to learn about the two-way interaction of communication.

Ask Me for It

Materials

3–4 objects that are familiar to the baby, such as a ball, spoon, cup, small stuffed animal, doll, block, toy car, etc.

This activity is appropriate for babies who are crawling or walking.

What to Do with the Baby

- While the baby is watching, name each object as you place it on the floor or a low table.
- Take the baby to another part of the room.
- Ask the baby to bring you one of the objects: "Go find the blue ball and bring it to me."
- When the baby brings you the object, say thank you and let the baby know you are pleased: "Thank you, Josh! You found the blue ball and gave it to me."
- Repeat with the remaining objects.

How This Helps the Baby

This activity helps the baby make the association between an object and the object's name. It will also help the baby learn action words such as *go, get, give, find,* and *bring.*

Where's . . . ?

Materials

None

Do this activity when other people familiar to the baby are in the room.

What to Do with the Baby

- Hold the baby in your arms or on your lap.
- Say, "Where is Molly? Can you point to Molly?"
- Point to the person and say, "There's Molly."
- Repeat with the other people in the room, including yourself and the baby: "Where's Ronnie? Can you point to Ronnie? You are Ronnie."

How This Helps the Baby

Babies recognize the important people in their lives. This activity helps them make the connection between the people and the names of the people.

Moving: Activities

Chapter 4

Moving: Activities That Support Babies' Physical Development

When you consider the progress a baby makes in the area of large-muscle development in just fifteen months, you have a sense of the phenomenal overall growth that takes place in this short span of a child's life. The baby has little control of her muscles when she is a newborn. At around two or three months, she gains neck control. Between four and seven months, she learns to roll over, which is followed by crawling, standing up, and walking. Two facts are important here: large-muscle development does not necessarily happen at those exact ages or in that order for every child; and babies need practice to help strengthen their motor skills.

A few years ago, we were asked to observe a ten-month-old baby in a child care setting. The caregiver was worried about the baby's large-muscle development. During the first several months of the baby's life, the parents had been worried about their child's safety. As a result, they had kept their child almost exclusively in a frontpack or backpack. The result was quite profound. The baby, at ten months, could barely roll over or raise her chest off the floor when lying on her stomach. This demonstrates how important it is for caregivers to talk with parents about ways to encourage their child's large-muscle development.

Physical development typically happens from the head downward to the rest of the body and from the center of the body outward to the hands and feet. If you have different ages of babies in your care, you can observe this growth. A newborn is all thrusting legs and arms with clenched fists and a wobbly head. If you unlock a newborn's tiny fist, unfold his fingers, and place a rattle in it, he will probably clutch the rattle, give a few jerky movements, and drop it. His awareness of the rattle and his eye-hand coordination that allows him to continue grasping it have not yet developed. Now, watch a seven- or eight-month-old and see her roll from her back to her stomach, grasp and transfer objects from one hand to the other, sit up, and crawl. Pretty amazing what a baby learns in less than a year!

Infant massage, swimming lessons for babies, and even a few simple bicycle exercises while diapering can all help in a baby's large-muscle development. In the activities on the following pages, we suggest you consider doing some of them outdoors as well as indoors. It is easy to get wrapped up in the time and safety factors involved with bringing babies outdoors that we forget about the benefits. The climate, landscape and openness, and wildlife of the outdoors can offer wonderful learning and development opportunities for babies. In *Caring Spaces, Learning Places*, Jim Greenman offers many suggestions for outdoor environments and activities for babies that you can create from simple materials like different sizes of cardboard boxes and fiberboard barrels.

This chapter offers activities that can help babies develop their muscles.

Crinkle Play Mat

Materials

Paper city or road map
Tape

Unfold the map and cover the edges with tape to avoid paper cuts.

What to Do with the Baby

- Spread the unfolded map on a carpeted floor.
- Place the baby on the map on his tummy or back.
- Either sit near the map or on it with the baby.
- Play with the baby in the same ways you would if he were on a blanket. Rattles, balls, and stuffed animals will encourage movement.

How This Helps the Baby

Babies spend a lot of time lying on their backs or tummies. This paper play mat adds an interesting crinkle noise to baby's smallest movements.

Baby Aerobics

Materials

Musical recordings (optional)

What to Do with the Baby

- You can do these aerobics to music that has varying tempos and rhythms, or without music.
- Lay the baby on her back on a blanket on the floor or on her bed.
- Gently lift her arms up and then lower them.
- Repeat several times.
- Lift and lower the baby's arms one at a time.
- Repeat several times.
- Gently move the baby's legs up and down, then apart and back together.
- Repeat several times.
- Talk to the baby while she goes through her exercise routine: "Your arms go up and then they come down. You are getting so strong."

How This Helps the Baby

This activity helps babies build strength and coordination important for learning to crawl and walk.

Rolling Rattle

Materials

Empty cylindrical salt or oatmeal box
Jingle bells, buttons, or other items to use as noisemakers
Strapping tape

If using a salt box, pull out the metal spout to put small items like buttons or jingle bells inside. Place noisemakers inside the salt or oatmeal box and securely tape shut the opening. This is a wonderful floor toy. You can vary the activity by wrapping the box with a layer of quilt batting and covering it all with fabric to make a soft rolling rattle.

What to Do with the Baby

- Give the baby (and yourself) the freedom and space to move around.
- Place the baby on his tummy to encourage him to hold up his head. (Newborns will lay their heads on one side or the other.)
- Place the toy where the baby must reach for it or crawl toward it.
- Help the baby rock the toy back and forth.
- Copy what the baby does with the toy.

How This Helps the Baby

The shape makes this toy move in an interesting way, and the sound it makes when it rolls will attract the baby's attention. The baby can practice many skills with this simple toy, including touching, tapping, pushing, pulling, and grasping. The activity will encourage the baby to hold up his head and try to grab or roll over in order to reach the toy. Older babies may attempt to creep or pull themselves toward the toy if it is out of reach.

Jingle Blocks

Materials

Pint-size milk cartons, two per block
Large jingle bells
Newspaper
Strapping tape
Con-Tact paper (optional)

Hint: A dusting of baking soda inside the cartons after they have dried will help neutralize any odor.

You will need two milk cartons for each block. Wash the milk cartons thoroughly and let them dry. Remove the tops from two of the milk cartons. Place a jingle bell inside one carton and lightly stuff newspaper around the bell. Push the open ends of the two cartons together and secure the boxes together with strapping tape. The blocks may be covered with cheerful Con-Tact paper to make them more durable.

Safety Note: Check each block on a regular basis to make sure there is no danger of the jingle bell coming out of it and posing a choking hazard.

What to Do with the Baby

- Hand a block to the baby or help a younger baby hold it with both hands.
- Hold a block just out of the baby's reach and shake it to encourage the baby to try to grasp the jingling toy.
- Talk to the baby about what she is doing with the blocks: "You helped the block make its jingle, jingle, jingle sound."
- Stack two or three blocks and show an older baby how to knock them over.

How This Helps the Baby

A younger baby will tune into the sound the interesting block-shaped toys make when they are shaken or dropped. An older baby will learn about cause and effect as she recognizes her ability to make the blocks jingle.

Eggstra Fun

Materials

Large two-sectioned, plastic egg
2–3 large plastic buttons or poker chips
8-inch piece of cloth ribbon
Epoxy glue

Place the buttons or poker chips in one section of the egg. Tie a knot in one end of the ribbon. Follow the instructions for using the epoxy. Spread the epoxy on the rim of the egg halves and, just before pressing the sections together, slip just the knotted end of the ribbon inside. (There should only be a 6-inch length of ribbon showing.) Let the glue dry thoroughly.

Safety Note: Check the egg rattle on a regular basis to make sure there is no danger of the buttons or poker chips coming out and posing a choking hazard.

What to Do with the Baby

- Hand the egg-rattle to the baby.
- When the rattle falls or rolls out of reach, help the baby retrieve it with the attached ribbon.
- While the baby is lying on her back, shake the egg-rattle near one side of the baby's head until she looks. Help her to roll over and grasp the rattle.

How This Helps the Baby

Babies experience their environment with their ears, eyes, and hands. At this age, they like to hold and shake a toy. This activity will help babies practice using their eyes and hands together as they lean forward to grasp the egg.

Baby Blocks

Materials

Small jewelry gift boxes (squares and rectangles)
Con-Tact paper

Gather 3 or 4 boxes of various shapes and sizes. Cover each box with brightly colored Con-Tact paper.

What to Do with the Baby

- While the baby is watching, stack the blocks and knock them over.
- Repeat.
- Talk about what you are doing with the blocks: "We can build a tower with the blocks and then knock them down."
- Sound effects will attract and keep the baby's attention on the activity.
- Encourage the baby to join in the fun. Help him with the stacking and crashing, if necessary.

How This Helps the Baby

Blocks are wonderful for helping babies with their small-muscle development and eye-hand coordination. These blocks are small enough for tiny hands to easily grasp and maneuver. The Con-Tact paper cover makes them durable and mouthable.

Twin Tubes

Materials

2–3 empty paper-towel and/or toilet-paper tubes
Con-Tact paper

Cover the outsides of the tubes with Con-Tact paper.

What to Do with the Baby

- Hand one of the tubes to the baby, holding it slightly out of reach so she will want to grasp it.
- While the baby is holding a tube, hand her another tube and watch what happens. Will she take the second tube into her empty hand? Will the first tube be dropped in favor of the new offering?
- How will the baby deal with the introduction of a third tube?
- Extend the game by helping the baby bang two of the tubes together.
- While using one of the tubes to gently tap different parts of the baby's body, say, "This is Shannon's leg, arm, tummy," and so on.

How This Helps the Baby

The activity will support the development of a baby's eye-hand coordination and problem-solving skills. Playing with the tubes encourages the baby to practice grasping and holding an object.

Thundering Cookie Sheet

Materials

Lightweight aluminum cookie sheet

What to Do with the Baby

- Hold the cookie sheet up to the baby's feet while he is kicking his legs.
- The cookie sheet will thump and rattle in response to the baby's kicking. When the baby kicks, he is rewarded with a thunderous sound. Smile and laugh to show your own delight in hearing the reverberation.
- Describe what the baby is doing: "Your kicking feet are making a big noise."

How This Helps the Baby

A baby is very interested in watching his feet wiggle and kick. He is learning about his own body and how he can cause parts of it to move. This activity encourages the baby to exercise leg muscles to strengthen them in preparation for standing, crawling, and walking.

Rolling Pop Bottle

Materials

2 empty two-liter plastic soda-pop bottles
A variety of small toys (small balls, tiny stuffed toys, etc.)
Heavy-duty scissors or hacksaw
Fine sandpaper
Epoxy glue
Cloth tape or strapping tape

Wash the bottles and remove the labels. Cut off the top one-third of each bottle using the scissors or the saw. Discard the tops and smooth the cut edges with fine sandpaper. (An emery board works well for this job, too, if you don't have sandpaper.) Place the toys inside one of the bottles. Following the instructions for using the epoxy, glue the cut ends of the bottles together to form an enclosed capsule. For extra security, tape the seam closed with strapping tape or cloth tape.

What to Do with the Baby

- Sit on the floor with the baby.
- Show the baby the rolling pop bottle and name the objects that are enclosed: "Can you see the little red ball inside the bottle?"
- Put the toy on the floor and roll it away from you. Retrieve it.
- Place the rolling pop bottle just out of the baby's reach. Encourage her to reach for the toy or crawl toward it.

How This Helps the Baby

This toy can help a baby who is just learning to crawl. It encourages her to move forward on her tummy or hands and knees. Crawling helps coordinate the movement of the arms and legs on both sides of the body, which is important for the development of that major coordination skill—walking.

I Tug, You Tug

Materials

10-inch piece of heavy yarn (or a clean adult sock)

What to Do with the Baby

- Sit on the floor with the baby.
- Help him grasp one end of the yarn as you hold onto the other end.
- Gently pull the yarn toward you.
- Encourage the baby to pull his end of the yarn: "You are so strong. I have to hold on tightly to my end of the yarn to play this game with you."
- Tug back and forth, varying how hard you pull on your end of the yarn.

How This Helps the Baby

The baby is practicing grasping and letting go of objects while playing this cause-and-effect game with you.

Tunnel of Fun

Materials

Large cardboard box or packing carton
Strapping tape
Soft toy
Scissors or knife

Choose a box that is large enough to create a tunnel for the baby to easily crawl through. Use the scissors or knife to remove the flaps from both ends of the box. Cover the cut edges with strapping tape.

What to Do with the Baby

- Set the tunnel in an area where the baby likes to crawl.
- Place a favorite soft toy inside the tunnel.
- Encourage the baby to crawl to the toy inside the tunnel.
- Place the toy just outside the opposite side of the tunnel from the baby.
- Position yourself on the floor next to the toy.
- Encourage the baby to crawl through the tunnel to get to the toy and you.
- At first, the baby may not be interested in the tunnel. Repeat the activity a couple of times, but if there is still no interest, try again later.
- Move the tunnel to a safe, grassy area in your outdoor space and repeat the activity.

How This Helps the Baby

Crawling is an important skill for babies to master before they walk. It helps them coordinate the arm and leg movements on both sides of the body.

Cup o' People

Materials

6- or 8-ounce empty yogurt container with transparent lid
Small photograph of someone significant in baby's life
Several pieces of shaped, plastic confetti (teddy bears, hearts, stars, or other shapes)
Glue and/or strapping tape

Wash and dry the yogurt container. Cut the photograph into a circle that will fit the bottom inside of the yogurt container. Glue or tape the picture in place. Add the confetti for "shake appeal" and secure the lid to the container with nontoxic glue or strapping tape.

To vary the activity, attach a cut-to-size piece of shiny Mylar instead of a photo to the inside of the transparent lid, add the confetti, and secure the lid to the container. This creates a safe mirror toy.

What to Do with the Baby

- Hand the Cup-o'-People toy to the baby.
- Point to and say the names of the people in the photograph and explain what they are doing—laughing, smiling, and so on.
- Help the baby shake the toy to keep her attention focused on the photograph.

How This Helps the Baby

Babies are very interested in their world and the people who care for them. This shaking toy encourages eye-hand coordination and supports the development of the baby's social awareness. The baby recognizes familiar faces, including her own.

Drawer Explore

Materials

Empty drawer (or cupboard)

Safe, unbreakable objects (small pots and pans with lids, plastic containers, wooden spoon, clean dishcloth or towel, unused household rubber glove, etc.)

Instead of putting child-resistant locks on all drawers and cupboards in your home or facility, keep one available to the babies. Empty one low drawer and fill it with safe, unbreakable objects. Objects that bang, clang, and clatter are especially fun.

Safety Note: If you choose to use a kitchen drawer or cupboard for this activity, do not allow the child access to the drawer or cupboard when you are cooking or cleaning in the room, and might be using materials that would be dangerous to the baby.

What to Do with the Baby

- Encourage the baby to open the drawer. Help him if necessary.
- Persuade the baby to explore the different objects he finds in the drawer.
- Observe what the baby does with the objects. He may bang the pot with the spoon, stack the plastic containers, play peek-a-boo with the towel, or simply be content to empty and fill the drawer over and over again.
- Talk to the baby about the different objects and support his efforts to explore them in his own way: "Are you stacking the red bowl inside the blue bowl?"
- Occasionally, add a new object or two to the drawer.

How This Helps the Baby

Your child care environment should be filled with interesting, accessible objects for babies to explore to their hearts' content. This activity does that and supports small-muscle development and eye-hand coordination.

Baby's First Pull-Toy

Materials

Fabric ribbon
Small stuffed toy
Rattle

Securely tie one end of the ribbon to the stuffed toy and the other end of the ribbon to the rattle. Make sure there is no more than a 6-inch length of ribbon between the toy and rattle so it cannot become wrapped around the baby's neck.

What to Do with the Baby

● Place the pull-toy just out of the baby's reach and encourage her to grasp one part of it and pull it toward her.

● Observe her reaction as she notices the other toy comes to her, as well.

● Talk to the baby about what she is doing: "You pulled the rattle and the bear came to visit you too."

How This Helps the Baby

Babies like toys with ribbons or strings that allow the toys to be dragged or carried around. Grasping and pulling the toys helps the baby practice eye-hand coordination. She will enjoy the cause-and-effect action as she sets the toys in motion.

Rattle Activity Box

Materials

5–6 homemade or commercially made rattles
Sturdy box or basket

Place the rattles in the box or basket.

What to Do with the Baby

- Sit with the baby on the floor and set the box of rattles next to her.
- Choose a rattle from the box and shake it. Say, "Look, Rebecca, this box is filled with lots of toys that make noise."
- Put the rattle back in the box and encourage the baby to grab a rattle and give it a shake. She may even grab two.

How This Helps the Baby

Rattles are great cause-and-effect toys that encourage babies to practice grasping and holding onto objects.

Nesting and Stacking

Materials

3 plastic lids from aerosol cans; lids should nest inside one another (Use lids from canned whipped cream, cooking spray, or other food items, not ones from hairspray or bug spray.)

Wash the lids in soapy water and dry them.
You can vary the activity by using empty, clean milk cartons of various sizes, cut so they are cube-shaped and of similar height. However, square containers are more difficult than circular ones for babies to nest together.

What to Do with the Baby

- Sit on the floor with the baby.
- Place the plastic lids on the floor by the baby and let him enjoy exploring them.
- Place the large lid, open side up, in front of the baby.
- Place the medium lid, open side up, inside the large lid.
- Place the small lid, open side up, inside the medium lid.
- Talk about what you are doing and what the baby is seeing: "This smaller lid fits inside the larger lid."
- Help the baby fit the lids inside one another. Encourage all his attempts to nest the lids.

Repeat the nesting activity in a different manner:

- Place the large lid, open side down, in front of the baby.
- Stack the medium lid, open side down, on top of the large lid.
- Stack the small lid, open side down, on top of the medium lid.
- Talk about what you are doing and what the baby is seeing: "This smaller lid stands on top of the larger lid."
- Help the baby stack the lids on top of one another. Encourage all his attempts to stack the lids.
- Repeat the stacking activity.

How This Helps the Baby

This activity gives the baby the opportunity to develop his eye-hand coordination. It is also a premath experience that helps the baby learn about graduated differences in sizes and what comes first, second, and third. This math concept is called *seriation*.

Noisy Sock Ball

Materials

Clean sock (A colorful, patterned sock is more interesting than a plain white one.)
Cellophane (not plastic food-storage wrap)
Scissors
Needle and thread

If the cellophane is in one large piece, cut it into smaller squares or strips. Stuff the toe of the sock with crumpled cellophane pieces until you have a ball shape. Leaving about 1½ to 2 inches above the ball, cut off the remaining portion of the sock. Securely sew the ball closed using the needle and thread.

What to Do with the Baby

- Sit so you are facing the baby.
- Show the baby the ball.
- Squeeze the ball several times so the baby can hear the crinkle sound it makes.
- Describe the sound: "The ball sounds all crinkly and crunchy."
- Hand the ball to the baby and help her make the crinkling sound.
- Gently take the ball from the baby and toss it a short distance. Say, "I can throw the ball."
- Retrieve the ball and throw it again.
- Hand the ball to the baby and encourage her to throw it, or help her throw it. Say, "Terri can throw the ball."
- Repeat as long as the baby shows an interest in the game.

How This Helps the Baby

Babies enjoy dropping and throwing objects. This activity helps babies develop eye-hand coordination and encourages their exploration of the concept of cause-and-effect. The crinkling sound adds interest to the ball, and the baby will extend her play with it.

Jiggle Jug

Materials

Clean milk or juice jug with handle
6–8 old-fashioned wooden clothespins (not the spring type)

What to Do with the Baby

- While the baby is watching, drop the clothespins into the jug.
- Shake the jug.
- Observe the baby's reaction.
- Shake the clothespins out of the jug, and again drop them into the jug.
- A very young baby will enjoy the jug as a giant rattle. An older baby may attempt to empty the clothespins out of the jug and put them back in. It will be much easier for the baby to fill the jug than to empty it.

How This Helps the Baby

The baby will enjoy shaking (or kicking) the jug. Add some background music and encourage the baby to shake the jug in time to the rhythm. This activity helps the baby learn about cause and effect and develop eye-hand coordination.

Here I Come!
I'm Going to Get You!

Materials

None

What to Do with the Baby

- Place the baby where he likes to crawl.
- Get down on your hands and knees.
- Crawl toward the baby and say, "Here I come. I'm going to get you!"
- Let the baby move ahead of you.
- Gently grab him and say, "Gotcha!"
- Repeat, repeat, repeat.
- Encourage the baby to try to catch you—and let him.
- Vary this activity by rolling a ball away from the two of you. Chase the ball together.

How This Helps the Baby

Babies like to have adults crawl with them. This activity helps the baby develop and practice crawling.

Pouring

Materials

2 paper or plastic cups
Dry cereal (Oat rings work well.)

What to Do with the Baby

- Fill one of the cups with a few pieces of the cereal.
- Seat the baby in her high chair or sit with her on the floor.
- Show the baby how to pour the cereal from one cup into the other cup.
- Help the baby pour the cereal back into the first cup.
- Let the baby try to pour the cereal by herself. She can always eat what she spills.

How This Helps the Baby

This activity allows the baby to practice eye-hand coordination. She will need this coordination when she is ready to learn how to pour liquids.

Leg Tunnel

Materials

None

What to Do with the Baby

- Stand with your legs apart.
- Place the baby on his hands and knees and help him crawl between your legs.
- Turn the baby around and help him crawl back through your legs.
- Talk to the baby about what he is doing: "Ben's crawling through the leg tunnel and coming out the other side."
- Have a coworker or older child stand with legs apart behind or in front of you to make a longer tunnel for the baby to crawl through.

How This Helps the Baby

This crawling game encourages the baby to practice moving his body through small spaces.

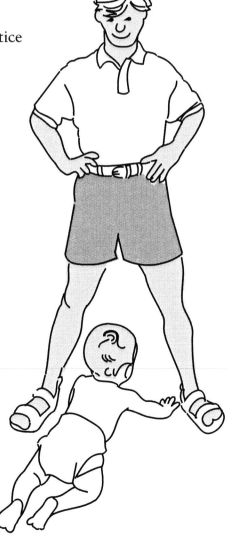

Choo-Choo Pull-Toy

Materials

2 empty cylindrical oatmeal boxes with lids
Heavy string or yarn
Nail or scissors
Strapping tape
2 extra-large jingle bells (optional)

Work with a long piece of string or yarn. (You will cut it to a safe length when the toy is completed.) Use the nail or scissors to punch a hole in the center of one of the lids. Thread one end of the string through the hole on the top of the lid and make a knot on the underside of the lid. Place a couple strips of tape over the knot so it won't pull out. If you want the pull-toy to make noise, put a jingle bell inside the box. Place the lid on the box and tape it in place. About 6 inches from the lid, tie another knot in the string.

Punch a hole in the center of the bottom of the other oatmeal box. Thread the string (already attached to the first box) up through the hole in the bottom of the second box. Pull until the knot you just tied rests against the bottom of the box. Place a couple of pieces of tape over the knot on the bottom of the second box. Place a jingle bell inside the box if you want the pull-toy to make noise. Punch a hole in the center of the remaining lid and thread the string through the hole from the inside. Place the lid on the box and tape it in place. Trim the string so it is less than 6 inches long, and tie a large knot in the end.

What to Do with the Baby

- Sit on the floor with the baby.
- Pull the end of the string to show the baby how the Choo-Choo Pull-Toy moves.
- Help the baby grasp the end of the string and pull the toy.
- Babies who are able to walk can pull the Choo-Choo Pull-Toy from a standing position.

How This Helps the Baby

This activity encourages the baby to practice eye-hand coordination and/or walking skills to make the pull-toy move and jingle.

Magnet Board

Materials

6 metal lids from frozen juice cans (the ones with smooth edges that you can pop off the cardboard cans)

6 colorful stickers

Flat magnets (Craft stores sell a variety of magnets in different sizes and shapes. Purchase ones that are large enough to not pose a choking hazard.)

Epoxy glue

Cookie sheet (or metal tray)

Wash and dry the lids and check them for any rough edges. Attach a sticker to the top side of each lid. Using the epoxy, glue a magnet to the bottom of each lid. Let the glue dry thoroughly.

Safety Note: Check the magnets on a regular basis to make sure they are still firmly attached to the lids.

Vary the activity by gluing cut-to-size photographs to the tops of the juice can lids. Or you can expand the game by adding more lids and duplicating stickers to make it a matching game.

What to Do with the Baby

- Place the lids, magnet side down, on the flat surface of the cookie sheet.
- Place the cookie sheet on the floor or a table.
- Sit on the floor with the baby or hold her in your lap as you sit at the table.
- Describe the colors and shapes of the stickers.
- Show the baby how you can move the lids by sliding them across the surface of the cookie sheet or picking them up and moving them to a different location.
- Hand a lid to the baby and help her place it back on the cookie sheet.
- Encourage the baby to pick up a lid that is attached to the cookie sheet.

How This Helps the Baby

Babies enjoy picking things up and exploring new things with their fingers. The magnet board encourages them to practice reaching for and maneuvering objects. While the "magic" of magnetism is a concept they will not understand for quite some time, babies will enjoy the cause-and-effect features of this activity. They may even discover on their own that the lids will not only stick to the cookie sheet but to each other.

Sticky Pictures

Materials

Con-Tact paper
Tape
Lids from small yogurt containers
Photographs or magazine pictures
Scissors
Glue

Remove the paper backing from a 1- to 3-foot-long piece of Con-Tact paper and use tape to attach it to the wall at baby-height, sticky side out. Cut out photographs or magazine pictures to fit the tops of the yogurt cup lids. Glue the pictures to the lids. Let the glue dry thoroughly.

What to Do with the Baby

- Position the baby in front of the Con-Tact paper—the "sticky wall."
- Stick the picture lids to the sticky wall and then remove them.
- Encourage the baby to stick a picture lid on the wall. Help him if necessary.
- Continue with the remaining lids.
- Encourage the baby to remove a lid and stick it somewhere else on the wall.
- Talk about the pictures, the sound the lids make when you remove them, and how it feels to touch the sticky wall: "The picture makes a funny sound when you pull it off the sticky wall."

How This Helps the Baby

This is a wonderful small-muscle activity. It helps the baby practice grasping with his thumb and finger as he peels the lids from the sticky wall. If you use photographs of the baby, the other children in your care, or their families and pets, you turn this into a social/emotional activity, as well.

Scribble Art

Materials

Large piece of paper or newsprint
Masking tape
Fat crayon (nontoxic)

Tape the paper to the top of a low table so it won't slide around. This also allows the baby
to use the crayon with either hand. Remove the paper covering from the crayon.

What to Do with the Baby

- Seat the baby at the table or allow her to stand.
- Offer the crayon to the baby and let her explore it. She may want to feel it, put it in her mouth, or show it to you.
- Describe the crayon: "The crayon is blue and smooth."
- Gently place the crayon in the baby's hand. She will probably hold it in her fist.
- Show her how to make a mark on the paper. Say, "You made a blue mark on the paper with the blue crayon."

How This Helps the Baby

Babies will need a lot of practice holding crayons and pencils. The baby will start out
palming the crayon. As her small-muscle skills increase, she will eventually learn to hold
the crayon with her thumb and fingers. It also takes some practice for her to learn to apply
enough pressure on the crayon to make a mark.

Climber

Materials

Phone book
Masking or strapping tape
Con-Tact paper

Wrap tape around the phone book to help the book retain its shape, then cover the entire phone book with Con-Tact paper.

What to Do with the Baby

- Place the phone book in a carpeted area of the room where the baby likes to play. Observe her reaction.
- Encourage the nonwalking baby to crawl on top of and over the phone book: "You can crawl up and then you can crawl down."
- You can help the baby who is walking to step up on the phone book and step or jump down. Assist the baby by holding him under his arms or by the hand.

How This Helps the Baby

Babies are going to become climbers, so it is a good idea to have a lot of low, safe things around for them to climb on, over, and around. This activity helps babies practice balancing and adjusting their bodies to remain upright. When you lie on the floor, you too will become something the babies love to crawl on top of or over!

Play Ball

Materials

Small and large balls

What to Do with the Baby

- Seat the baby on the floor and help her place her legs so they are open and outstretched.
- Sit directly across from the baby and place your own legs so they are open and outstretched.
- Roll the ball to the baby.
- Encourage the baby to catch the ball and roll it back to you.
- Repeat, repeat, repeat.
- Use a different size ball and repeat the activity.

How This Helps the Baby

Babies this age are usually very good at reaching and grasping objects. This activity helps the baby practice catching and holding an object and then releasing it from her hand. It takes a while for the baby to learn to relax her hand and fingers enough to let go of an object. The ball may go flying as the baby perfects this skill, so move the activity away from other children and use soft indoor balls that won't hurt anyone if they accidentally get tossed farther than the baby intends.

Soft Toss

Materials

Fabric
Scissors
Needle and thread or sewing machine
Cotton balls or quilt batting
Large box or laundry basket

Cut six 8-inch squares of fabric. Stack two of the squares and sew three of the sides together using small hand stitches or the sewing machine. Turn the square inside out. Stuff it with cotton balls or batting to make a puffy pillow shape. Stitch the opening securely closed by hand or on the sewing machine. Repeat with the remaining squares.

What to Do with the Baby

- Set up this activity in an area where the baby can safely throw the squares.
- Have the baby stand away (but not too far) from the box or basket.
- Hand the baby one of the soft squares and encourage him to toss it into the box or basket: "Can you throw this into the box from where you are standing?"
- Help him toss the square if necessary.
- Hand the baby another square and encourage him to keep tossing.
- Show the baby how to take the squares out of the box or basket.
- Repeat, repeat, repeat.

How This Helps the Baby

This activity gives the baby a chance to practice grasping and then releasing an object. The stuffed square is a soft, light version of a beanbag. The box or basket gives the baby a target to hit so he can work on eye-hand coordination.

Kick Ball

Materials

Plastic beach ball

What to Do with the Baby

- Do this activity in a large, open space, or move it outdoors.
- Stand facing the baby with about 4 or 5 feet between you.
- Gently kick the beach ball so it slowly rolls toward the baby and stops at her feet.
- The baby may want to use her hands to move the ball, but encourage her to use her foot and leg to kick it back to you. If necessary, hold on to her hands to help her keep her balance as she kicks the ball.

How This Helps the Baby

This activity allows the baby to practice briefly balancing on one leg. A beach ball is much easier to kick than a smaller ball.

Feeling: Activities

Chapter 5

Feeling: Activities That Nurture Babies' Emotional and Social Development

Do babies have feelings? The answer is yes! A baby has a repertoire of feelings even as a tiny infant. Babies smile and wiggle to show they like playing with you. They frown or cry when you stop paying attention to them or playing with them. Sometimes babies laugh with a belly laugh. From the beginning, emotions play a major role in a child's learning and development.

Emotions create a chemical release that fixes memories. For example, when you read a story to a baby in a soothing voice while the baby is snuggled up with you in a rocking chair, the baby remembers the feeling of being read to this way. It motivates the baby to engage with you in the reading, imitate it, and, eventually, master the many skills that reading entails. The same thing happens when you touch and comfort babies when they are having a tantrum. The repeated contact helps babies gain control, and that memory of assurance stays with them as they grow to gain self-control. Just the opposite happens, by the way, when a baby is repeatedly ignored. In that case, the baby becomes increasingly anxious and despondent or angry. So it's clear that you are creating lifelong emotional building blocks for the child in these fifteen months!

Babies are learning about social interactions and how things work. In infancy, babies begin to tell the difference between people they know and don't know. Young babies may get distressed if a stranger tries to hold them or look them in the eyes. If you are a consistent, loving, and skilled caregiver, you have probably won the trust of the babies in your care. You are much more interesting than any of their toys when you smile and talk with them or play peek-a-boo. Their reliance on you makes you want to be sure that you respect their trust. Let them know when you are leaving and greet them when you come back (please note our activities in the following pages addressing this concern). In building trust, it is important to create a partnership in caregiving with their parents (also referred to in the introduction).

As babies get older, their capacity for a two-way conversation (social engagement) becomes more sophisticated. Babies begin to signal their needs and look to you for your reaction. For example, six-month-old babies usually reach out to be picked up, and when they are picked up, they coo with gratitude. By the time babies are fifteen months old, they take your hand and walk you over to show you the toy they want.

Babies interact with one another, but they are doing it out of curiosity and exploration rather than socialization. If you have cared for babies for even a short length of time, you know that these interactions are not always conducive to life in groups! You remember—very quickly—that babies are discovering the world through their senses as they bite, squeeze, and pull one another. You need to watch and monitor this interaction so no one gets hurt, while making sure babies still have the opportunity to learn how to be with one another.

On the following pages are activities that help babies with their emotional development.

Walking Fingers

Materials

None

What to Do with the Baby

- Lay the baby on her back in your lap, on the floor, or in her crib.
- Wiggle your hand to focus the baby's attention on your fingers.
- Slowly walk your fingers toward the baby and end by gently poking the baby in the tummy.
- Walk your fingers up the baby's arm and end by gently poking the baby in the tummy or tapping her under the chin.

How This Helps the Baby

Babies love the social interaction of this game. They learn to anticipate the tummy poke and may start to giggle before you even get there.

Silly Mouth

Materials

None

What to Do with the Baby

- Hold the baby in your lap so you are facing each other.
- Make silly shapes and sounds with your mouth and lips: smack your lips, make a "raspberry" sound, stick out your tongue, wiggle your tongue, make a popping sound with your lips, blow a kiss, smile, frown, make a loud kissing sound, and so on.
- The baby will laugh at your silliness and may try to imitate you.
- Repeat the baby's favorite silly sounds and faces.

How This Helps the Baby

This is a fun communication game to play with babies.

Soothing a Crying Baby

Materials

None

What to Do with the Baby

- Check the obvious things first: Does the baby need burping, to be fed, a clean diaper, or a new sleeping position?
- Reduce the stimulation: Dim the lights, move to a quieter room, check to make sure there are not too many toys or too many people around. Overstimulation is often a problem in a large child care setting.
- Provide monotonous background noises, such as a ticking clock, a running washing machine, or quiet music.
- Help the baby bring his hand or pacifier to his mouth to suck.
- Firmly wrap (but not too tightly) the baby in a blanket and walk or bounce the baby as you hold him against your chest.
- Lay the baby across your lap and stroke him or gently move your knees from side to side as you hum to him.
- Hold the baby's hands in yours against his chest.

How This Helps the Baby

We've all felt a little frustrated and helpless when we've had to deal with the incessant crying of a baby. It is often a matter of trial and error to find what works to soothe the baby.

You and Me

Materials

None

What to Do with the Baby

- When a baby starts to have some control of head movements, lie on your back on the floor and put the baby on your chest.
- Let her look into your face, pull your hair, and grab your nose.

How This Helps the Baby

In these early months of life, babies learn how to engage one-on-one with another person. They learn best about socialization by experimenting through their senses. Give babies access to your body so they can gaze into your eyes.

Ahh-boo!

Materials

None

What to Do with the Baby

- Put the baby on your lap with the baby's face looking into yours. Smile and say "ahh-boo!" as you gently bump your forehead to his.
- Repeat as long as the baby seems to be enjoying it.

How This Helps the Baby

The one-on-one engagement and attention this activity provides gives the baby confidence to move to the next stages of emotional and social development.

Up and Down You Go

Materials

None

What to Do with the Baby

- Hold the baby on your lap so he is facing you.
- Place your hands around the baby's chest and up under his arms.
- Make eye contact and gently raise the baby so his head is a little above yours.
- Smile and say, "Up you go."
- Slowly lower the baby back down to your lap and say, "Down you go."
- Repeat, repeat, repeat.

How This Helps the Baby

This activity lets babies know by your voice and facial expressions that you are happy to be playing with them. It encourages them to express their own excitement and joy.

Sweet Tummy

Materials

None

What to Do with the Baby

- Three or four quick kisses on a baby's bare tummy usually sends the baby into belly laughter!
- You can shake your head as you vibrate the baby's tummy with your lips—like a horse does when it's tired.

How This Helps the Baby

Ah, simple pleasures! This is another activity that promotes the emotional power of one-on-one engagement and social development.

Peek-a-Boo

Materials

Scarf or baby blanket (optional)

What to Do with the Baby

- Position the baby so she is facing you.
- Put your hands in front of your face, then quickly remove them as you say, "Peek-a-boo."
- Repeat. Repeat. Repeat.
- Hold a scarf (or blanket) in front of your face. Lower the scarf and say, "Peek-a-boo."
- Repeat. Repeat. Repeat.
- Place the scarf over the baby's head and pull off the scarf as you say, "Peek-a-boo."
- Repeat. Repeat. Repeat.
- Place the scarf over the baby's head and help her pull it off. Say, "Peek-a-boo."
- Repeat. Repeat. Repeat.

As a baby gets closer to fifteen months and becomes mobile, you can play hide and seek. Hide behind a piece of furniture or equipment with part of you in plain view. You can say, "Where am I? Here I am, Mary!" Soon she will come after you—laughing with anticipation.

How This Helps the Baby

This is probably the oldest baby game around because it hardly ever fails to bring a smile to babies' faces or elicit giggles from them—and from the caregiver. Babies learn some important lessons while enjoying this one-on-one play time. First, they learn that not being able to see an object doesn't mean it is not still there. This is called *object permanence*. And, because you repeat the action sequence again and again, babies learn to anticipate what will happen next.

Now You See It, Now You Don't

Materials

Small toy
Cardboard or heavy paper

What to Do with the Baby

- Sit down at a table and hold the baby on your lap.
- Let the baby hold the toy for a minute.
- Place the toy on the table.
- Put the cardboard in front of the toy so it is out of sight. Say, "I'm hiding the toy behind the cardboard. We can't see it."
- Lift the cardboard up and down or move it from side to side so the toy can be seen and then not seen by the baby.
- The baby may try to knock over the cardboard to get to the toy or lose interest in the activity until the toy reappears.
- Talk to the baby about what you are doing and what the baby is seeing: "Now we can see the truck, now we don't see the truck. Where did it go?"

How This Helps the Baby

At around six to eight months of age, babies begin to understand that not being able to see an object doesn't mean it is not still there. They are able to hold an image of a particular object in their minds even when the object is no longer visible.

Dance with Me

Materials

Musical recordings (a variety of tempos and rhythms)

What to Do with the Baby

- Pick up the baby and say, "Won't you dance with me?"
- Hold the baby on your hip and dance around the room to the music.
- If the baby can walk, you can hold on to both of the baby's hands and sway to the music together.

How This Helps the Baby

Babies will enjoy being close to you as you both move around the room to the music.

Making New Friends

Materials

Toy

Do this activity when you want to introduce the baby to someone new—perhaps a new staff member, or the parent of a newly enrolled child.

What to Do with the Baby

- Hold the baby securely in your arms.
- Face the new person, smile, and say, "Hello, Carol."
- Extend your hand to shake the hand of the new person.
- Chat for a minute with the new person while the baby watches and listens.
- Introduce the baby to the new person. "Shawna, this is Carol."
- Have the new person offer a toy to the baby. The baby may take the toy, touch it, or just look at it.
- If the baby is willing to go to the new person, stay close by.

How This Helps the Baby

Very young babies are usually willing to go to any adult. Older babies, although curious, are much more cautious around unfamiliar people—even close relatives. Respect babies' needs for some extra time to feel comfortable and learn about new people in their worlds.

Give and Take

Materials

Toy

What to Do with the Baby

- Sit in front of a baby and hand the baby a toy, saying, "Here you go, Molly."
- Then reach out your hand with your palm up and say, "Please give it to me, Molly."
- If the baby doesn't hand it back to you, gently take it with a "Thank you very much, Molly."
- Repeat the sequence a couple of times.

How This Helps the Baby

Babies are learning the give-and-take interchange between people. This exercise is a first step in learning how to take turns.

Sprinklers

Materials

Various plastic containers (margarine tub, cup, bowl, film canister, shampoo bottle, etc.)
Nail or ice pick
Dishpan
Water
Shower curtain (optional)

Thoroughly wash the containers. Use a sharp nail or an ice pick to punch 6–8 holes in the side of each container. Create different patterns with the holes in each container. You may want to leave a couple of the containers without holes. Fill the dishpan about half full of room-temperature water.

Safety Note: Never leave the baby alone during this activity. Empty the water from the dishpan and the containers when you have completed the activity.

What to Do with the Baby

- Cover the floor with the shower curtain or move this activity outdoors.
- Place the dishpan of water on the floor.
- Sit down on the floor next to the dishpan.
- Hold the baby in your lap or place the baby on the floor next to you.
- Show the baby one of the plastic-container "sprinklers."
- Dip a sprinkler into the dishpan of water and let it fill up past the holes.
- Lift the sprinkler out of the water and watch the water pour out of the holes.
- Help the baby put his hand out to feel the water as it sprinkles from the container.
- Help the baby fill the sprinkler again and hold onto it as the water escapes.
- Let the baby play with the container in the water.
- Repeat with the other containers. If you have containers without holes, introduce them into the activity and observe the baby's reaction.
- Help the baby fill the containers without holes with water, then pour it back into the dishpan. Fill one container with water, then pour the water into another container. Ask the baby to pour water from his container into yours.

How This Helps the Baby

Most babies find water play very soothing. This activity gives them an early lesson about the properties of liquids. It demonstrates the ways that water can change shape and take the shape of the container that holds it.

Resources

Publications

Arcedolo, Linda, and Susan Goodwyn. *Baby Minds: Brain-Building Games Your Baby Will Love.* New York: Bantam, 2000.

Bales, D. "Building Baby's Brain: The Basics," article published by the University of Georgia College of Family and Consumer Sciences, 1998.

Begley, S. "How to Build a Baby's Brain," *Newsweek*, 1997, pp. 28–32.

Cooperative Extension Systems of the University of Idaho and University of Nebraska. "Achieving High Quality Child Care," October 1993. This excellent series is currently being republished. It consists of a video and a participant information packet made up of 25 reader-friendly short booklets on six child care program areas (for example, one booklet is dedicated to parent-information forms, another is on how to change a diaper). Agriculture Publications, 208-885-7982.

Greenman, Jim. *Caring Spaces, Learning Places: Children's Environments That Work.* Redmond, Washington: Exchange Press, 1988.

Greenman, Jim, and Anne Stonehouse. *Prime Times: A Handbook for Excellence in Infant and Toddler Programs.* St. Paul: Redleaf Press, 1996.

I Am Your Child Foundation. *The First Years Last Forever,* video and booklet, 888-447-3400, www.iamyourchild.org. Created by the Reiner Foundation and the Families and Work Institute.

National Institute of Child Health and Human Development (NICHD). *Study of Early Child Care.* Bethesda, Maryland: NICHD, 1998.

Shore, R. "Rethinking the Brain: New Insights into Early Development." New York: Families and Work Institute, 1997.

Special 2000 Edition. "Your Child." *Newsweek*, Fall/Winter 2000.

Special Report. "How a Child's Brain Develops." *Time*, February 3, 1997.

Organizations

These organizations have Web sites that pertain to infant and toddler care:

Early Head Start
http://www.ehsnrc.org/

I Am Your Child
http://www.iamyourchild.org/

National Association for Child Care Resource and Referral Agencies (NACCRRA)
http://www.naccrra.net/

National Association for the Education of Young Children (NAEYC)
http://www.naeyc.org/

National Child Care Information Center (NCCIC)
http://nccic.org/

National Governors Association
http://www.nga.org/

Northwest Regional Education Laboratory (NWREL)
http://www.nwrel.org/

Redleaf Press
http://www.redleafpress.org/

WestEd Lab: Center for Child and Family Studies
http://www.wested.org/

Zero to Three
http://www.zerotothree.org/